FIRST
FUN
ATLAS

First published in 2001 by Miles Kelly Publishing Ltd
Bardfield Centre, Great Bardfield, Essex CM7 4SL

2 4 6 8 10 9 7 5 3 1

Copyright © 2001 Miles Kelly Publishing Ltd

ISBN 1-902947-86-X

Printed in Hong Kong

Author
Andrew Langley
Editorial Director
Paula Borton
Art Director
Clare Sleven
Project Editor
Neil de Cort
Editorial Assistant
Nicola Sail
Designer
Venita Kidwai
Artwork Commissioning
Lesley Cartlidge
Consultant
Clive Carpenter
Indexing
Jane Parker

PHOTOGRAPHIC CREDITS
18 (B/L) Marc Meuench/ CORBIS; 21 (B/R) Michael T. Sedam/
CORBIS; 28 (T/L) Pawel Libera/ CORBIS; 28 (C/R) Richard
Hamilton Smith/ CORBIS; 30 (T/L) O.Alamany & E Vicens/
CORBIS; 36 (B/R) Charles O'Rear/ CORBIS; 39 (T/R)
Jack Fields/ CORBIS; 41 (T/R) Charles & Josette Lenars/
CORBIS; 41 (B/R) Paul A. Souders/ CORBIS; 42 (T/L) Galen
Rowell/ CORBIS.

ACKNOWLEDGEMENTS
The Publishers would like to thank the following artists who
have contributed to this book:
Jim Channell/ Bernard Thornton   Terry Riley
Chris Forsey   Ted Smart
Terry Gabbey/ AFA   Guy Smith/ Mainline Design
Mick Loates/ Linden Artists

Maps by Martin Sanders

www.mileskelly.net
info@mileskelly.net

FIRST FUN ATLAS

Andrew Langley

Miles Kelly
PUBLISHING

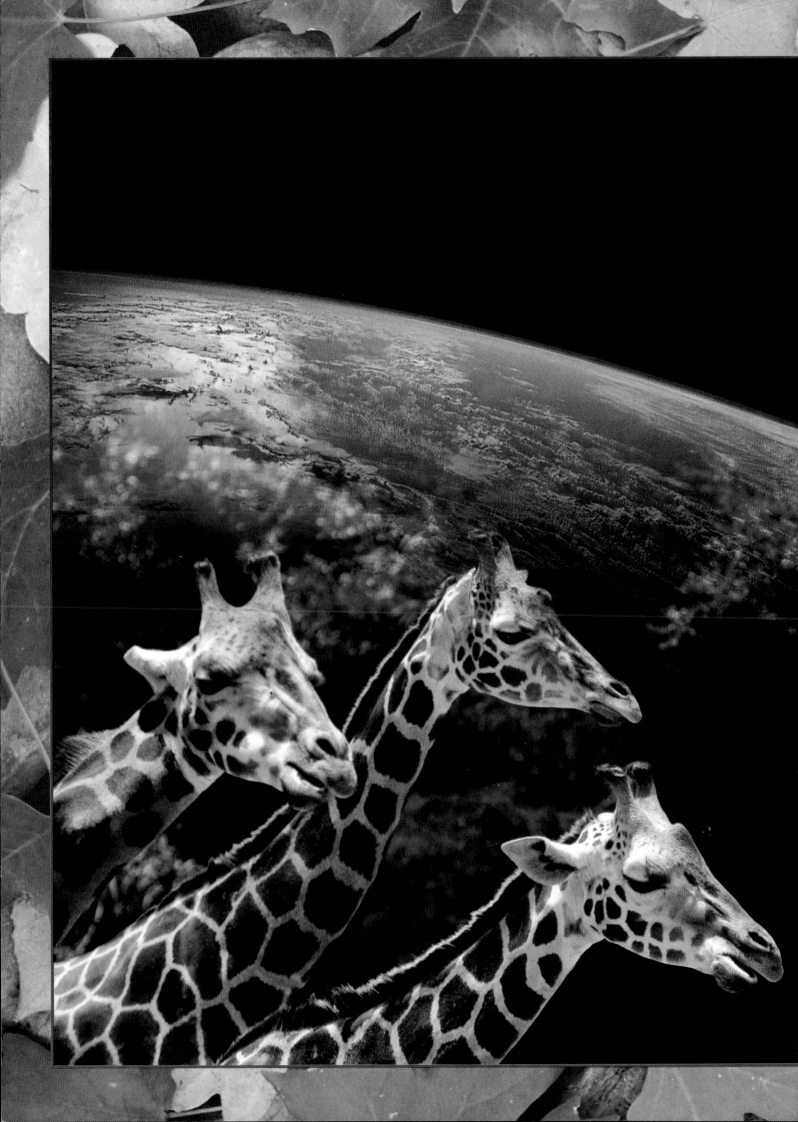

Contents

Earth in space

Imagine you are far out in space.
You turn and look back at the planet we call Earth. What does it look like? It is round like a ball, and coloured, mostly blue and green with smudges of white.

It is also small — much smaller than most of the other planets that are near us. Some of these are huge, and could swallow up the Earth many times over. But, even bigger, is the Sun, a giant mass of fire and flame that is the brightest thing in our small corner of space. The Earth gets all its heat, light and energy from the Sun.

If you watched for long enough, you would see that the Earth does not stay in one place. It moves in a big circle around the Sun. This circle is called Earth's orbit. One whole journey around the Sun takes a year, or just over 365 days.

▲ The Moon

The Earth has a rocky ball, the Moon, that circles around it as it moves through space. It is one-quarter the size of the Earth. The Moon's surface is full of great holes called craters.

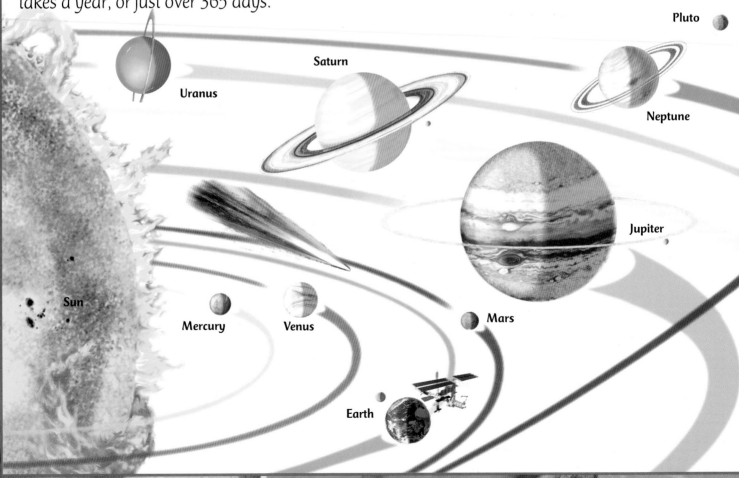

Pluto

Saturn

Uranus

Neptune

Jupiter

Sun

Mercury

Venus

Mars

Earth

▲ Spinning in space

Earth does not just move through space, it also spins round, like a top. Imagine a line drawn through the middle of the Earth from top to bottom. The Earth spins around that line, making a complete turn every 24 hours – a day and a night.

▼ Parts of the Earth

The Earth is split up into lots of layers, almost like an onion. If you could cut open the Earth you would be able to see all the different layers inside. The outside layer is called the crust. This is up to 50 kilometres deep in some places, but compared to the whole Earth it is very small. If the Earth was an apple, the crust would be as thick as its skin! The next layer is called the mantle. This is a layer of soft, hot rock that is nearly 2,900 kilometres thick. After this is the outer core which is made up mostly of molten metals, iron and nickel. In the middle is the inner core, where temperatures reach as high as 7,000 degrees Celsius.

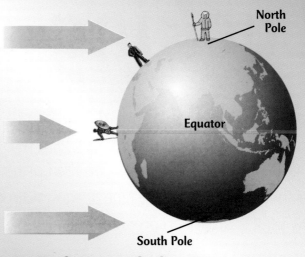

▲ Poles and the Equator

At the very top of the world is the North Pole. At the bottom is the South Pole. And halfway between is an imaginary line called the Equator. The Equator is the part of the world nearest to the Sun, so it is always hot. The poles are furthest from the Sun, so they are cold.

The seasons

The Earth tilts over slightly as it spins around. This means that for half of the year the top half of the Earth is tilted towards the Sun. This gives us the warmer seasons of spring and summer. When the Earth is tilted away from the Sun, we have the colder seasons of autumn and winter.

▶ Day and night

The Earth is constantly spinning like a top. At any time, the Sun only shines on one half of the Earth's surface. As the Earth spins around, the sunshine moves onto a different part of the surface. On the side of the Earth where the Sun is shining, it is light and day. On the side of the Earth that is facing away from the Sun, it is dark and night.

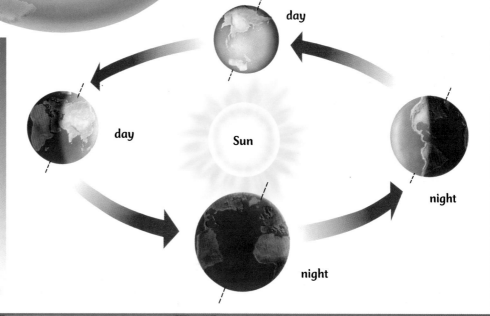

Looking at the Earth

How can we know what the Earth looks like? If you were an astronaut you could see it very well from your spacecraft. But the rest of us have to stay on the Earth's surface. We can't see the shape of a whole coastline or mountain or river. We can't tell how far it is across an ocean or between two cities.

Instead, we look at a map of the Earth. A map is a diagram, which shows where things are on the Earth's surface. Each kind of feature has its own sign or symbol. Symbols come in many different lines, colours and shapes to show rivers, mountains, towns, and so on.

There are many kinds of map. Some show the main features, using different colours for rainforest, desert or highland areas. Others use boundary lines and colours to show how the world is divided up into countries and states. Maps can be big or small. A map can show the whole world – or just your street!

▲ **Continent map**
This is the continent of Oceania. You can see Australia, New Zealand, and the small islands in the Pacific Ocean.

▶ **Country map**
Maps like this one of Australia show you where different towns and cities are. They will also tell you where to find other land features, such as mountains, rivers, lakes and deserts.

◀ Eye in the sky

Modern mapmakers use photographs taken from high in the sky by satellites or aircraft. Special machines transfer the shapes from the photos onto a sheet of paper. Mapmakers can also measure distances from these photographs. All this information is stored in a computer, which can then be used to control a drawing machine called a plotter.

▶ Round into flat

An exact map of the world would be a globe or sphere. But how do you draw this onto a flat piece of paper? One early method was to peel the Earth like an orange, then spread the peel out in sections (see the picture on the right). A better way was invented by Mercator in 1538. He wrapped a sheet of paper in a tube shape around a globe map, then copied the lines of the map onto it. When he unwrapped the tube, he had a flat map.

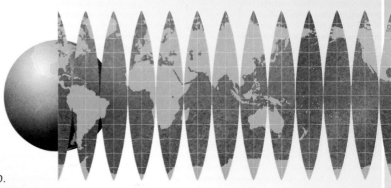

▼ Zooming in on Earth

The detail on Earth can be shown at different sizes. As you zoom in you can see more detail. Different maps are used to study the Earth. A globe shows the whole of the Earth. A state or county map will show you a small part of the Earth, while a street map will help you find your way around a city or town.

▲ World from afar

We cannot see all the countries on a globe because some are hidden. Here you can see Oceania, and some of Antarctica and Asia.

- Gulf of Carpentaria
- Coral Sea
- Great Sandy Desert
- **AUSTRALIA**
- Gibson Desert
- Great Victoria Desert
- Simpson Desert
- Nullarbor Plain
- Lake Eyre
- GREAT DIVIDING RANGE
- AN OCEAN
- or ea

▼ Making maps

As soon as people started exploring the world, they started drawing maps. Travellers brought back rough plans from different parts of the world. The first person to put these all together into a large map was the Greek, Ptolemy, about 1,900 years ago. But it still had many gaps – because large parts of the Earth were still unknown. Slowly, these gaps were filled in. The first complete world map did not appear until the last century.

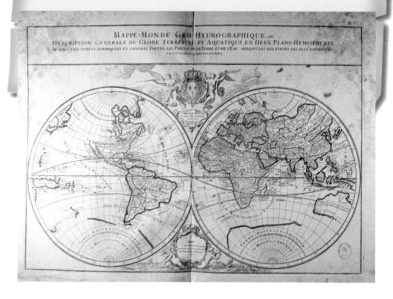

MAPPE-MONDE GEO-HYDROGRAPHIQUE ou
DESCRIPTION GENERALE DU GLOBE TERRESTRE ET AQUATIQUE EN DEUX PLANS-HEMISPHERES

▶ State map

Zooming in a bit more, you can see state or county details. You can also find the names and places of major cities and towns. You might use a map like this if you wanted to find out about the states of Australia. For example, from this map, can you tell in which state you would find the city of Brisbane?

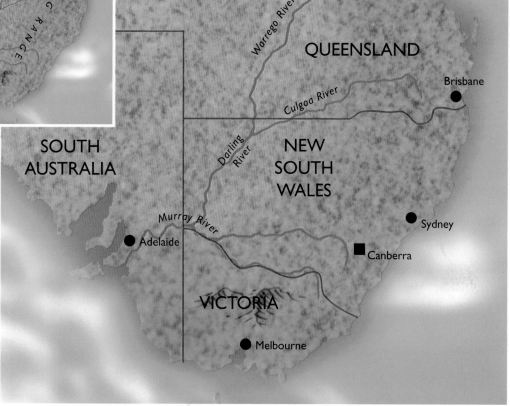

- Warrego River
- **QUEENSLAND**
- Brisbane
- Culgoa River
- Darling River
- **SOUTH AUSTRALIA**
- **NEW SOUTH WALES**
- Murray River
- Adelaide
- Sydney
- Canberra
- **VICTORIA**
- Melbourne

9

The world

Here is a map of the whole world – on two pages! It shows you all the main land areas of the world, and the oceans and seas. Can you see how much of the map is coloured blue? This is because there is so much water. Oceans, lakes, rivers and other water cover over two-thirds of the Earth's surface.

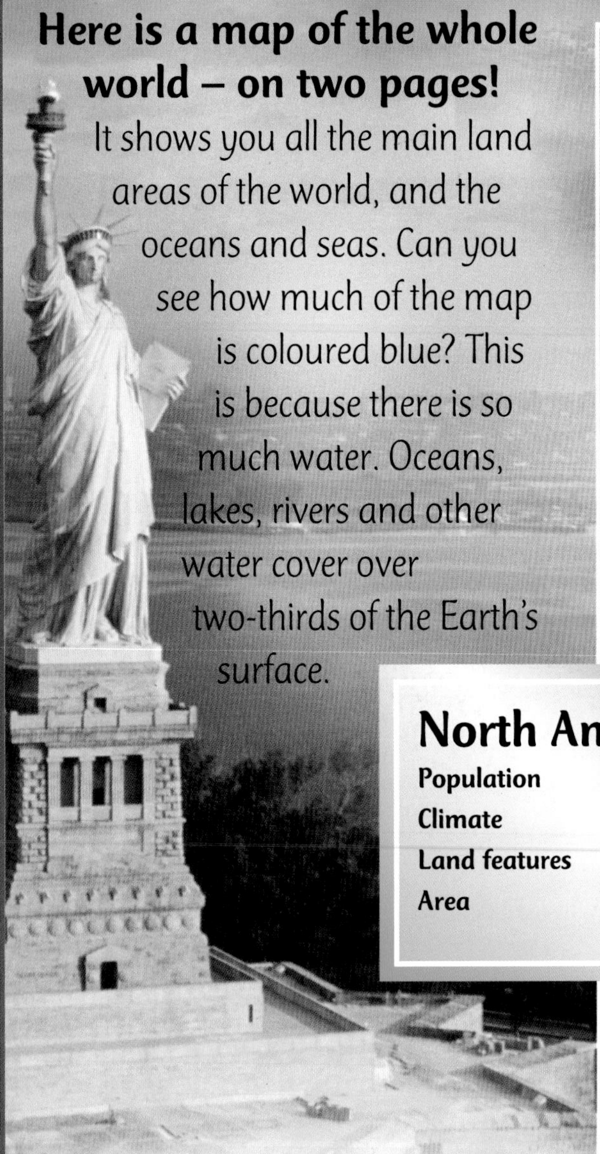

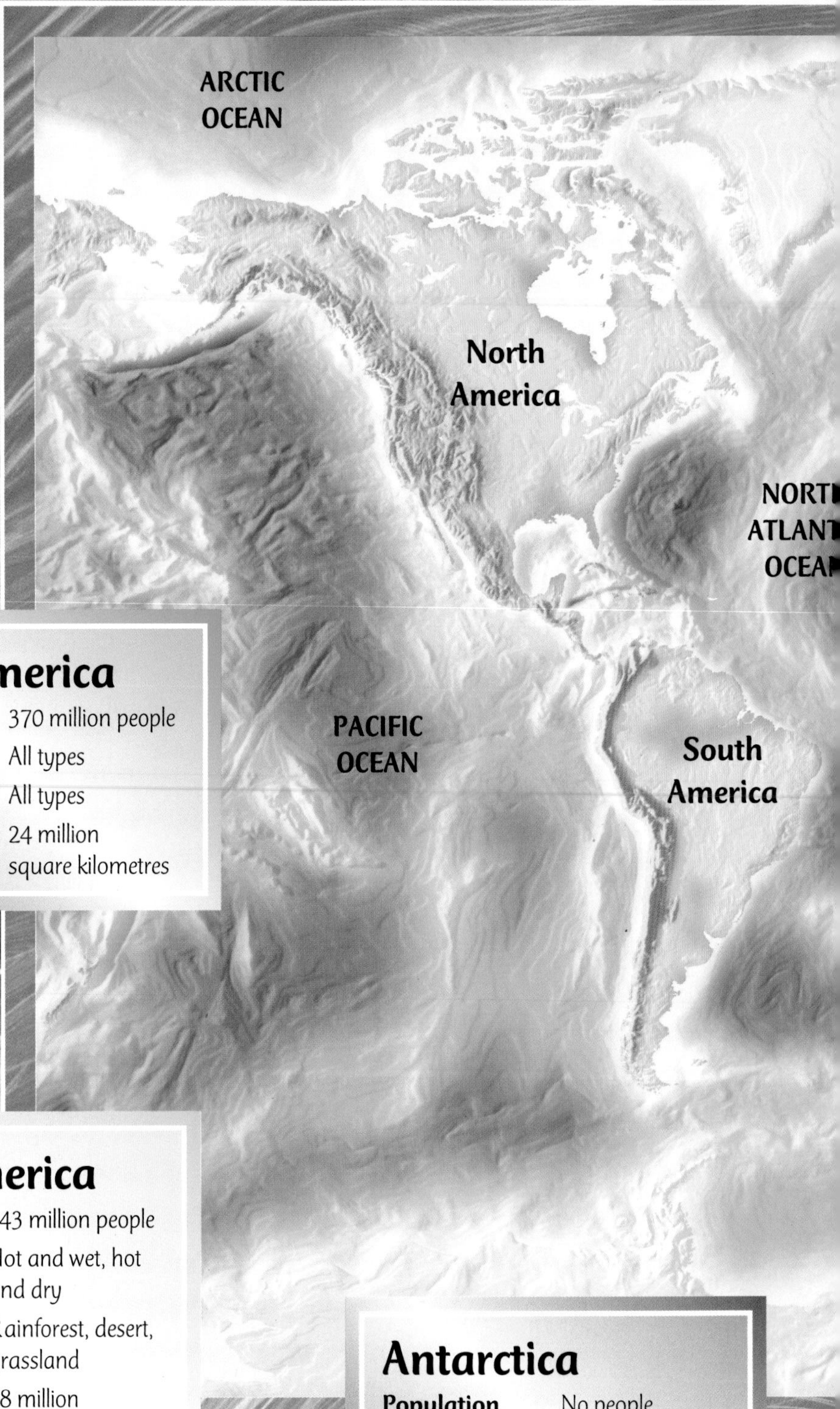

ARCTIC OCEAN

North America

NORTH ATLANTIC OCEAN

PACIFIC OCEAN

South America

North America

Population	370 million people
Climate	All types
Land features	All types
Area	24 million square kilometres

South America

Population	343 million people
Climate	Hot and wet, hot and dry
Land features	Rainforest, desert, grassland
Area	18 million square kilometres

Antarctica

Population	No people
Climate	Always very cold
Land features	Ice and snow
Area	14 million square kilometres

Europe
Population	700 million people
Climate	Mild
Land features	Plains, uplands, mountains
Area	10 million square kilometres

ARCTIC OCEAN

Asia

Europe

PACIFIC OCEAN

Africa

Asia
Population	3,497 million people
Climate	All types
Land features	All types
Area	44 million square kilometres

INDIAN OCEAN

Oceania

Oceania
Population	27 million people
Climate	Hot and dry, hot and wet, mild
Land features	Rainforest, desert, grassland
Area	18 million square kilometres

Antarctica

Africa
Population	660 million people
Climate	Hot and wet, hot and dry
Land features	Desert, rainforest, grassland
Area	30 million square kilometres

The continents

The land on the Earth's surface is split up into seven large areas that are called continents. Their names are North America, South America, Europe, Asia, Africa, Oceania and Antarctica. Some of these, such as Europe, are very crowded, while nobody at all lives permanently in Antarctica. Some are big blocks of land, while others, such as Oceania, are made up of thousands of islands — some enormous and some tiny.

If you look closely, you will see that some of the continents are joined together. North and South America are linked by a narrow strip of land, called an isthmus. Asia and Europe are really part of the same huge land mass, and only a narrow canal separates Africa from Asia.

North America

Africa

South America

Comparing countries in each continent

Do you know how many countries there are in each of the continents? Africa is not the largest continent, but it has the most countries — 53 in total. The continent with the fewest countries is South America — it has only 12.

53

47

44

23

14

12

Africa

Europe

Asia

North America

Oceania

South America

Highest and lowest temperatures

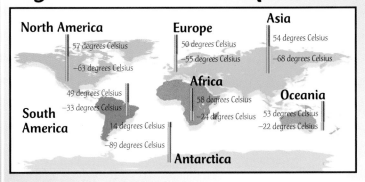

North America
57 degrees Celsius
−63 degrees Celsius

Europe
50 degrees Celsius
−55 degrees Celsius

Asia
54 degrees Celsius
−68 degrees Celsius

Africa
58 degrees Celsius
−24 degrees Celsius

49 degrees Celsius
−33 degrees Celsius

South America
14 degrees Celsius
−89 degrees Celsius

Oceania
53 degrees Celsius
−22 degrees Celsius

Antarctica

Europe

Asia

QUIZ

1. Which is the largest continent?
2. Which is the smallest continent?
3. Which continent has the most people?
4. Which is the coldest continent?
5. Which continent has the most countries?

Answers on page 48.

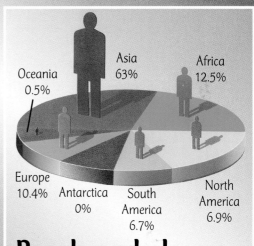

Oceania
0.5%

Asia
63%

Africa
12.5%

Europe
10.4%

Antarctica
0%

South
America
6.7%

North
America
6.9%

People and places

In the diagram above, the Earth is shown as a circle divided into the seven continents. It shows you how much bigger the area of Asia (purple) is than Oceania (orange). You can also see how many people live in each continent – the population. Sixty-three percent of the world's population lives in Asia while nobody lives in Antarctica.

Oceania

Antarctica

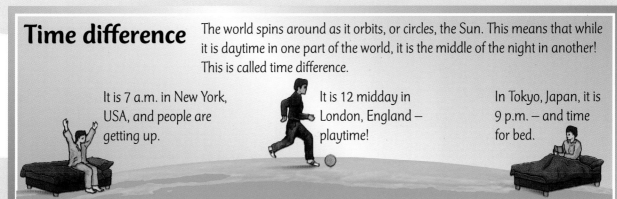

Time difference
The world spins around as it orbits, or circles, the Sun. This means that while it is daytime in one part of the world, it is the middle of the night in another! This is called time difference.

It is 7 a.m. in New York, USA, and people are getting up.

It is 12 midday in London, England – playtime!

In Tokyo, Japan, it is 9 p.m. – and time for bed.

Amazing Earth!

Did you know that around the world 250,000 new babies are born each day! Scientists have discovered 4,000 kinds of mammal, 21,000 kinds of fish and one million kinds of insect! The world is also full of amazing natural and man-made structures – some are shown here on these pages.

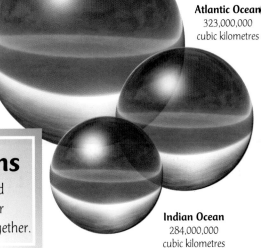

Pacific Ocean
696,000,000 cubic kilometres

Atlantic Ocean
323,000,000 cubic kilometres

Indian Ocean
284,000,000 cubic kilometres

▼ Largest deserts
The Sahara Desert is so large that it covers an area bigger than the USA!

▶ Biggest oceans
Large areas of salt water are called oceans. The Pacific Ocean is bigger than all of the Earth's land put together.

▼ Tallest structures
Here you can see some of the tallest structures in the world today. These are all self-supporting structures – they do not have anything else holding them up.

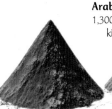

Arabian Desert
1,300,000 square kilometres

Kalahari Desert
520,000 square kilometres

Sahara Desert
9,269,000 square kilometres

Australian Desert
3,800,000 square kilometres

Gobi Desert
1,040,000 square kilometres

Features such as radio masts do not count in these measurements.

CN Tower
555 metres

Shanghai World Financial Center
460 metres

Petronas Towers
452 metres

Sears Tower
443 metres

Jin Mao Building
420 metres

World Trade Center
417 metres

Empire State Building
381 metres

Eiffel Tower
300 metres

Mount Everest
8,863 metres

Mount Aconcagua
6,959 metres

Mount McKinley
6,194 metres

Mount Kilimanjaro
5,894 metres

Mont Blanc
4,807 metres

Mount Cook
3,754 metres

◄ Biggest mountains

Mountains are the tallest things on Earth. Mount Cook, the smallest mountain shown here, is nearly six times taller than the world's tallest man-made structure!

► Longest rivers

The Earth's rivers travel for miles. The Nile River is long enough to stretch from the USA, across the Atlantic Ocean and into Europe!

Mississippi-Missouri River 3,779 kilometres
Volga River 3,531 kilometres
Murray River 2,520 kilometres
Chang Jiang River 6,300 kilometres
Amazon River 6,400 kilometres
Nile River 6,671 kilometres

▼ Tumbling water

The world's highest waterfalls make the tallest man-made buildings look tiny. The tallest building, the CN Tower (555 metres), is not even as tall as the third highest waterfall (579 metres)!

Angel Falls
972 metres

Giessbach Falls
604 metres

Sutherland Falls
579 metres

Ribbon Falls
491 metres

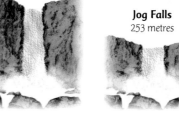

Jog Falls
253 metres

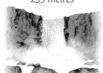

Victoria Falls
108 metres

Highest temperature ever recorded
58 degrees Celsius, Libya, Africa

Inhabited place with lowest average temperature
−11 degrees Celsius, Norilsk, Russia

Lowest temperature ever recorded
−89 degrees Celsius, Vostok, Antarctica

◄ Extreme temperatures

An egg that would freeze hard in the coldest place on Earth would get cooked in the hottest place!

► Oldest age

The oldest living thing – a creosote bush – has survived longer than 90 times the age of the oldest human!

Oldest human
122 years old

Oldest oak tree
1,000 years old

Oldest tree
Bristlecone pine –
4,000 years old

Oldest living thing
Creosote bush –
11,000 years old

Oldest animal
Giant tortoise – 192 years old

How to use the maps

Maps can look very puzzling. What are all those squiggly lines and strange colours and shapes? How can you fit a whole town or country onto one page?

You can read a map – just like you are reading this book now! Instead of letters and words, the map uses symbols and colour codes to give you information. Therefore to read a map you need to understand the symbols.

A feature on a map is much smaller than it is in real life. Maps show places at different sizes. So one centimetre on a map might represent one kilometre (that's 100,000 centimetres) on the ground.

Reading a book may open up whole new worlds – and so does reading a map. Just looking at the page of an atlas will help you to imagine jungles or mountains or deserts. You can work out journeys and measure how far it is from one place to another. Maps can even help you to discover why people's lives are so different.

Two types of maps

In your atlas you will find two different kinds of map. They are called physical and political maps. Physical maps show natural features, such as mountains and rivers, seas, lakes and islands. They would be there even if there were no people around. Political maps show countries and states, which would not exist without people.

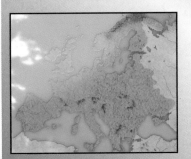
This physical map of Europe shows the rivers, mountains and seas.

This political map of Europe shows the countries in different colours.

▼ Physical map pages

Here you will find information about what the land in each continent looks like. Does it have mountains and rivers, deserts or rainforests? Can you tell if it is hot or cold? You will also discover amazing animals and wonderful natural places to visit.

Europe

Europe is the second smallest continent in the world – less than a quarter the size of Asia. Yet it is also the most crowded, with its population contained in 47 different countries.

Europe is able to support such a large number of people because it is lucky enough to have good farmland covering half of the continent. But there is less space for wildlife. The European brown bear is one of the few big animals to live in Europe.

There is a wide variety of birdlife, as well as smaller animals such as badgers, foxes, deer, hedgehogs, squirrels and wild boar.

△ Copper butterflies can live almost anywhere. They are tiny, growing to only 36 millimetres across their wings.

△ This fallow deer is guarding h[...] The white spots on their coats he[...] camouflage them amongst leave[...] they live. The fawn may stay wit[...] mother for more than a year.

△ A red fox's natural habitat is woodland, but many have ada[...] living in towns. They mainly hunt for food at night. They will ea[...] anything, from rabbits and earthworms to fish and apples.

Best of Europe

HOTTEST PLACE Seville in Spain recorded a high of 50 degrees Celsius in August 1881.

LARGEST SEA The Mediterranean Sea covers about 2,503,000 square kilometres.

LARG[...] Brit[...] isla[...] co[...] sq[...]

26

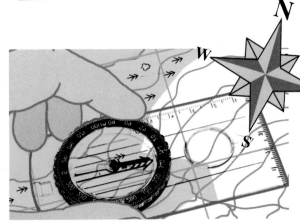

▼ Political map pages

Here you will find information about the places in each continent and facts about each country. You will also learn about the people who live there and what their lives are like.

▼ Grid lines

Can you see the numbers that run across the top of each page and the letters that run down the right of the border? These are called grid lines. You can use them to locate places on the map. For example, look for Belarus on the political map – its grid reference is D11. Trace a line with your finger across from D and down from 11 and you will find Belarus. See if you can find the grid references for Finland.

Europe
People and places

Europeans have changed the world.

Despite its small size, Europe has produced writers, artists...

The grebe is a water bird that dives underwater to catch food such as small fish, insects, snails and shrimps. It is the only bird that can dive whilst carrying its young.

Norwegian Sea

Barents Sea

North Sea

Baltic Sea

Lake Ladoga

Lake Onega

Volga River

Rhine River

Elbe River

Vistula River

Don River

Dnepr River

Seine River

Loire River

Bay of Biscay

PYRENEES

ALPS

CARPATHIANS

Danube River

Black Sea

Garonne River

Mediterranean Sea

The European peregrine falcon is the fastest animal in the world. It can dive at speeds of over 280 kilometres per hour, that is 75 metres a second.

LARGEST MAMMAL
Brown bears can grow to a height of 1.2 metres.

SLOWEST BIRD
The Eurasian woodcock can only fly very slowly, travelling 2 metres a second.

Greece is very popular with tourists. They visit the islands to enjoy the hot sunshine and visit the beautiful old buildings.

SWEDEN

FINLAND

NORWAY

Oslo Stockholm Helsinki

SCOTLAND

Edinburgh Tallinn **ESTONIA**

RUSSIA

IRELAND

Dublin

DENMARK

Copenhagen Riga **LATVIA**

Moscow

ENGLAND

WALES

Cardiff

LITHUANIA

Vilnius

Nicosia London

Brussels Berlin Minsk

BELGIUM **GERMANY** Warsaw **BELARUS**

Paris **POLAND** Kiev

SLOVAKIA **UKRAINE**

FRANCE Vienna Bratislava

AUSTRIA Budapest **MOLDOVA**

HUNGARY Chisinau

SPAIN **ROMANIA**

ITALY Belgrade Bucharest

YUGOSLAVIA **BULGARIA**

Rome Sofia

ALBANIA Tirana

GREECE

Athens

CYPRUS

QUIZ
Find the European countries, hidden in these jumbled up names.

OLD SCANT ANGRY ME
MARK END RAIN BIT
SIR USA CAR FEN

Answers on page 48

France is the most visited country in the world. The Eiffel Tower is one of its main attractions.

1. ANDORRA
   Andorra le Vella
2. BOSNIA-HERZEGOVINA
   Sarajevo
3. CROATIA
   Zagreb
4. CZECH REPUBLIC
   Prague
5. ICELAND
   Reykjavik
6. Kaliningrad
   (belongs to Russia)
7. LIECHTENSTEIN
   Vaduz
8. LUXEMBOURG
   Luxembourg
9. MACEDONIA
   Skopje
10. MALTA
    Valletta
11. MONACO
    Monaco
12. NETHERLANDS
    Amsterdam,
    The Hague
13. SAN MARINO
    San Marino
14. SLOVENIA
    Ljubljana
15. SWITZERLAND
    Bern
16. VATICAN CITY
    Vatican City

29

◄ Using a compass

A compass has a small needle in it that always points to the north (N). This helps you to find out where you are when studying a map. For example, it can help you to find which way you need to walk to get to a particular place.

Reading symbols on a map

Find out how to read the maps in this atlas by looking at the land colours and symbols used for the different features.

Desert **Grassland or forest** **Mountains**

POLAND
UKRAINE
National borders

HIMALAYAS
Mountain range

■ **Warsaw**
Capital city

Murray River
River

S A H A R A
D E S E R T
Desert

Lake Superior
Lake

North America

North America contains three huge countries!
These are Canada, the United States of America and Mexico. It also includes smaller countries in Central America and the islands in the Caribbean. This third biggest continent in the world stretches from the North Pole down to the Caribbean Sea. Here, a spindly strip of land containing the countries of Central America eventually joins South America.

In North America you can see cold white ice-caps, mountains, rainforests, deserts and forests – almost all the different kinds of land that can be seen anywhere in the world!

▼ An area of swampy land in the USA is home to the very rare Everglade jaguar – and lots of alligators too!

Col

◄ Kings Canyon is the deepest canyon in North America. Gradually worn away by the Kings River that flows through it, the canyon is 2,499 metres at its deepest point.

PACIFIC OCEAN

Best of North America

LARGEST GULF
The Gulf of Mexico covers 1,813,000 square kilometres.

LONGEST GORGE
The Grand Canyon, a valley with rocky sides, is 446 kilometres long.

LARGEST CRATER
Coon Butte Crater was made by a meteorite hitting the Earth. It is 1,265 metres across.

A
B
C
D
E
F
G

Great Bear Lake

Mackenzie River

Great Slave Lake

Hudson Bay

ATLANTIC OCEAN

ROCKY MOUNTAINS

Lake Winnipeg

Missouri River

Lake Superior

Lake Huron

St Lawrence River

Great Salt Lake

Lake Michigan

Lake Ontario

Lake Erie

Missouri River

Mississippi River

Rio Grande

Gulf of Mexico

Caribbean Sea

▲ Many animals live in the cold forests of Canada, including moose and bears. The moose is the largest deer in the world. Its antlers can grow up to two metres across.

HOTTEST PLACE
In Death Valley temperatures can rise as high as 57 degrees Celsius.

TALLEST LIVING THING
This giant redwood tree grows in America. It is 112 metres high.

LARGEST FRESHWATER LAKE
Lake Superior covers 82,260 square kilometres.

19

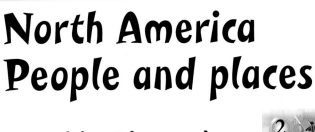

North America People and places

Some of the richest and poorest people live here. North America contains some of the world's largest cities, but also vast areas of remote land. The USA is the richest country in the world, and big cities such as Washington D.C. are centres of wealthy living. But many people in countries like Nicaragua and El Salvador in Central America are very poor.

The USA has become wealthy because it produces most of the world's silver, nickel and copper, as well as large amounts of coal, oil and gas.

By contrast, the people of Central America are not so lucky. The country does not have many natural resources, and the wealth they create is not evenly shared amongst everybody. Most people now live in cities, while the rest are small farmers growing just enough wheat, beans and rice to survive.

The Native American Indians lived in North America for a long time before anyone else arrived. Then people from Europe came to live there, and now there is a huge number of people who have come from many different places.

▲ Racing monster trucks like this one is a popular sport in Canada and the USA. The huge wheels and powerful engines mean that they can easily crush ordinary cars that get in their way!

QUIZ

Can you find out which cities are in the following squares by using the grid around the map?

D10, G9, E11, F11

Answers on page 48.

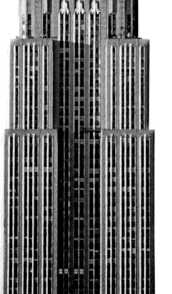

◄ The Empire State Building is one of the most famous places in the USA. Its 102 storeys rise to a height of 381 metres.

North America Facts

Biggest country Canada – 10,000,000 square kilometres

Biggest city population Mexico City – 17,000,000 people

Most TV sets USA – 81 out of 100 people own televisions

Fewest doctors Haiti – one doctor for every 7,140 people

Fewest TV sets Haiti – 5 out of 100 people own televisions

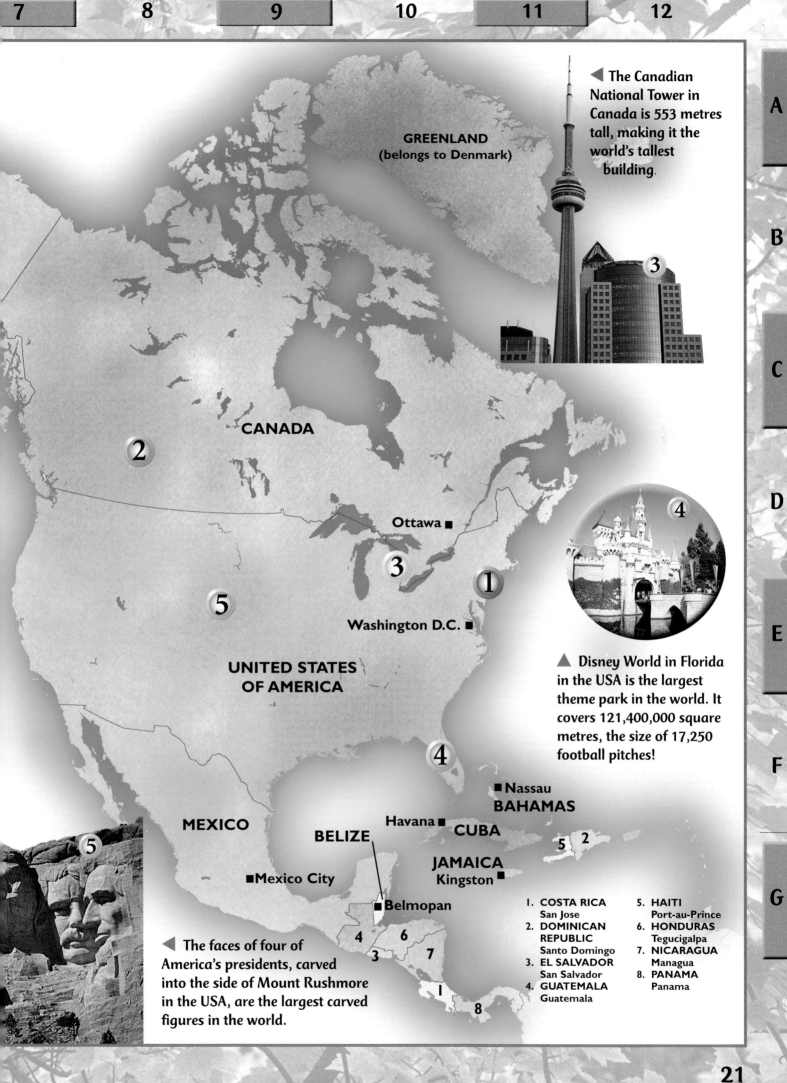

◄ The Canadian National Tower in Canada is 553 metres tall, making it the world's tallest building.

GREENLAND
(belongs to Denmark)

③

CANADA

②

Ottawa ■

③

①

Washington D.C. ■

④

▲ Disney World in Florida in the USA is the largest theme park in the world. It covers 121,400,000 square metres, the size of 17,250 football pitches!

UNITED STATES
OF AMERICA

⑤

④

■ Nassau
BAHAMAS

Havana ■ CUBA

MEXICO

BELIZE

⑤

JAMAICA
Kingston ■

■ Mexico City

⑤

⑤ ②

■ Belmopan

4 6

3 7

1. **COSTA RICA**
   San Jose
2. **DOMINICAN REPUBLIC**
   Santo Domingo
3. **EL SALVADOR**
   San Salvador
4. **GUATEMALA**
   Guatemala

5. **HAITI**
   Port-au-Prince
6. **HONDURAS**
   Tegucigalpa
7. **NICARAGUA**
   Managua
8. **PANAMA**
   Panama

◄ The faces of four of America's presidents, carved into the side of Mount Rushmore in the USA, are the largest carved figures in the world.

I

8

A
B
C
D
E
F
G

South America

South America means – jungle! The biggest tropical rainforest in the world covers an area ten times bigger than France. Through this forest winds the giant Amazon. It may be only the world's second longest river, but it carries two-thirds of the Earth's river water.

The continent contains many other marvels too. There are beautiful waterfalls, snowy mountaintops, and smoking volcanoes. It is a paradise for wildlife. A quarter of all known mammals live here, including the giant anteater and the vampire bat.

The rainforests are alive with beautiful birds, insects and animals. They also contain a staggering variety of plants, some of which give us vital medicines.

▲ The capybara is the largest rodent in the world. Rodents are animals like mice and rats, but the capybara can reach up to 1.4 metres in length!

▼ The anaconda, found in swampy river valleys in South America, is the widest snake in the world. It can measure 110 centimetres around its stomach!

Best of South America

LONGEST RIVER
The Amazon River runs for a total length of 6,750 kilometres.

HIGHEST WATERFALL
The water at Angel Falls plunges down a cliff 979 metres high.

DRIEST PLACE
The Atacama Desert has had no rain for over 400 years!

▶ The sloth is the slowest mammal on Earth. It normally moves at only 0.27 kilometres an hour – that's 15 seconds to move one metre!

Negro River

Amazon River

Purus River

Tapajos River

São Francisco

PACIFIC OCEAN

Lake Titicaca

Lake Poopo

Atacama Desert

ANDES

Parana River

Uruguay River

Parana River

ATLANTIC OCEAN

◀ Jaguars are the largest cats in South America. They can reach up to 2.2 metres in length, and weigh up to 90 kilograms.

▶ At the junction of two rivers, 275 waterfalls join together to form the spectacular Iguazú Falls.

ANDES

LONGEST RANGE
The Andes mountain chain runs for 7,200 kilometres. It is the longest in the world.

MOST PLANTS
The tropical rainforest contains more varieties of plant than anywhere else in the world.

| A |
| B |
| C |
| D |
| E |
| F |
| G |

South America
People and places

South America is the fourth largest continent but it has one of the smallest populations. This is because much of the land is difficult to live on, and the cutting down of the rainforests has forced native people to leave their homes.

Some of South America's farms are the biggest in the world and cover areas larger than some countries. However, most are small and farmers own or rent small plots of land, struggling to grow enough food to survive.

Three-quarters of the people in South America now live in towns and cities. Many of these people are very poor and cannot afford houses. They crowd into flimsy shelters on the outskirts of towns. Meanwhile a few South Americans are very wealthy. These are mainly the landowners, factory bosses and political leaders.

Until the Spanish and Portuguese invaded in about 1500 only native tribes lived in South America. Now most people are a mix of Native American and European.

► **This Bolivian woman is dressed in traditional clothes – blankets and a bowler hat. Life in rural Bolivia has not changed for many years.**

QUIZ

1. Can you count how many countries there are in South America?
2. Can you find the capital city of the largest country in South America?

Answers on page 48.

South America Facts

Smallest country Suriname – 163,820 square kilometres
Countries where most people live in cities Uruguay and Argentina – 89 out of 100 people live in cities
Country that produces most silver Peru – 14 percent of world total
Most TV sets Argentina – 22 out of 100 people own televisions
Fewest doctors Guyana – one doctor for every 6,220 people

◀ This beautiful statue of a bird with a snake is carved out of stone. It was made in Colombia about 2,000 years ago.

▶ Pipes like these are used by musicians who live in the Andes mountains.

VENEZUELA

■ Caracas

GUYANA

■ Georgetown

■ Paramaribo
FRENCH GUIANA
(belongs to France)

■ Bogota
COLOMBIA

SURINAME

■ Quito
ECUADOR

PERU

BRAZIL

■ Lima

■ Brasilia

■ La Paz
BOLIVIA

PARAGUAY

CHILE

■ Asunción

ARGENTINA

▼ Artists live in these brightly coloured flats in Buenos Aires, capital of Argentina. They have painted their houses in wonderful colours.

URUGUAY

■ Santiago

■ Buenos Aires

■ Montevideo

▼ Deforestation means cutting down forests. This is happening at an alarming rate. A total of 1,541,000 square kilometres was cleared between 1980 and 1990.

A
B
C
D
E
F
G

25

Europe

Europe is the second smallest continent in the world – less than a quarter the size of Asia. Yet it is also the most crowded, with its population contained in 47 different countries.

Europe is able to support such a large number of people because it is lucky enough to have good farmland covering half of the continent. But there is less space for wildlife. The European brown bear is one of the few big animals to live in Europe.

There is a wide variety of birdlife, as well as smaller animals such as badgers, foxes, deer, hedgehogs, squirrels and wild boar.

△ Copper butterflies can live almost anywhere. They are tiny, growing to only 36 millimetres across their wings.

△ This fallow deer is guarding her fawn. The white spots on their coats help camouflage them amongst leaves where they live. The fawn may stay with its mother for more than a year.

△ A red fox's natural habitat is woodland, but many have adapted to living in towns. They mainly hunt for food at night. They will eat almost anything, from rabbits and earthworms to fish and apples.

Best of Europe

HOTTEST PLACE
Seville in Spain recorded a high of 50 degrees Celsius in August 1881.

LARGEST SEA
The Mediterranean Sea covers about 2,503,000 square kilometres.

LARGEST ISLAND
Britain is the largest island in Europe, covering 218,041 square kilometres.

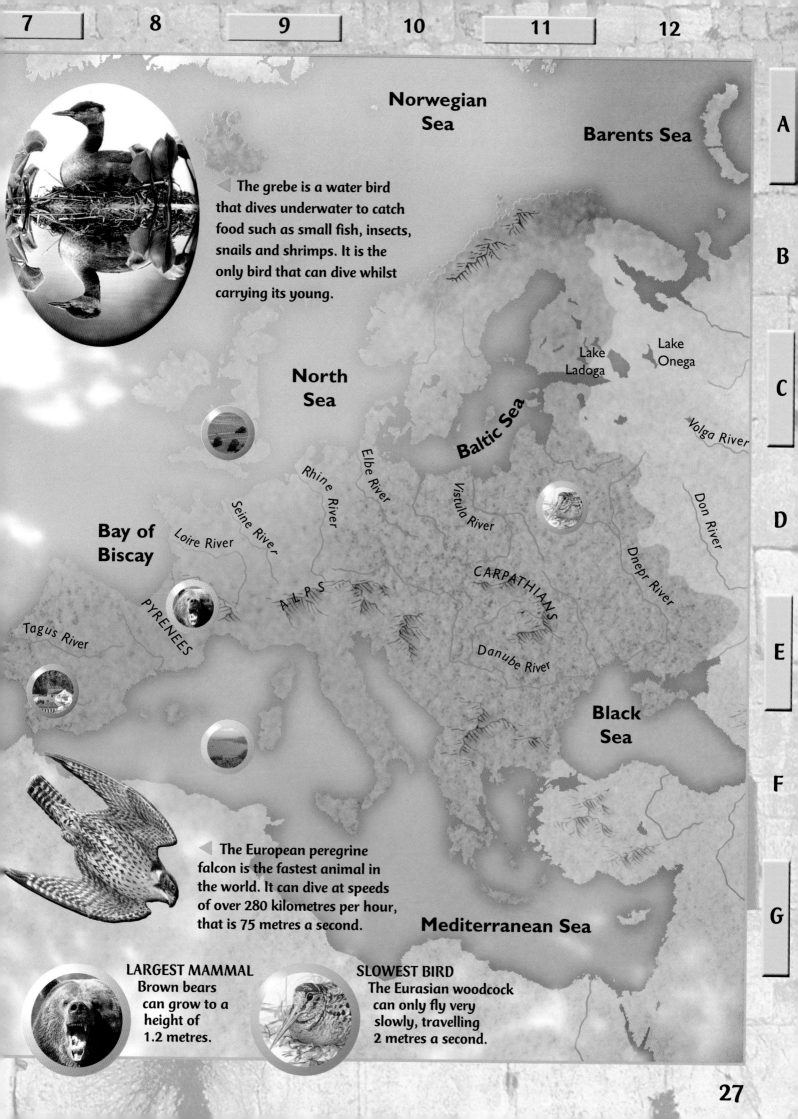

Norwegian
Sea

Barents Sea

The grebe is a water bird that dives underwater to catch food such as small fish, insects, snails and shrimps. It is the only bird that can dive whilst carrying its young.

North
Sea

Lake
Ladoga

Lake
Onega

Baltic Sea

Volga River

Rhine River

Elbe River

Vistula River

Don River

Bay of
Biscay

Seine River

Loire River

Dnepr River

CARPATHIANS

PYRENEES

A L P S

Tagus River

Danube River

Black
Sea

The European peregrine falcon is the fastest animal in the world. It can dive at speeds of over 280 kilometres per hour, that is 75 metres a second.

Mediterranean Sea

A B C D E F G

LARGEST MAMMAL
Brown bears can grow to a height of 1.2 metres.

SLOWEST BIRD
The Eurasian woodcock can only fly very slowly, travelling 2 metres a second.

27

5

Europe
People and places

Europeans have changed the world.

Despite its small size, Europe has produced writers, artists, scientists and explorers whose lives have influenced the rest of the world since the time of the ancient Greeks.

Most Europeans are descended from the tribes that roamed the area long ago. More than 70 different languages are spoken by the people living in Europe today. Over the last fifty years, many new settlers have come to Europe from Asia, Africa and the Caribbean.

Europe is a wealthy continent, with many modern kinds of industry. Today, Europe produces more manufactured goods than any other of the world's continents. Several countries, though, especially those in the east, remain poor.

Europe Facts

Biggest country

Russia – 3,900,000 square kilometres

(in Europe, the rest of Russia is in Asia)

Biggest city population

Paris, France – 8,900,000 people

Country where most people live in cities

Monaco – everybody lives in a city

Longest average length of life

San Marino – 81 years

▲ The London Eye is the world's highest observation wheel, standing at 136.1 metres. Views all over London can be seen from the top.

IRELAND

▲ Venice in Italy is a city built on water. Boats, such as these gondolas, are used to get around. They are moved with long poles that touch the bottom of the canals and drive the gondolas forward.

SPAIN

PORTUGAL

Madrid ■

■ Lisbon

◄ Neuschwanstein castle in Germany was the model for the Magic Kingdom castle in Walt Disney's theme park in the USA.

◀ Greece is very popular with tourists. They visit the islands to enjoy the hot sunshine and visit the beautiful old buildings.

QUIZ

Find the European countries, hidden in these jumbled up names.

OLD SCANT   ANGRY ME
MARK END   RAIN BIT
SIR USA   CAR FEN

Answers on page 48.

▲ France is the most visited country in the world. The Eiffel Tower is one of its main attractions.

SWEDEN

FINLAND

NORWAY

Oslo ■

Stockholm ■

Helsinki ■

■ Tallinn

RUSSIA

ESTONIA

SCOTLAND

■ Edinburgh

DENMARK

Riga ■

LATVIA

Moscow ■

blin

Copenhagen ■

LITHUANIA

Vilnius ■

ENGLAND

ALES

Cardiff

London

6

■ Minsk

BELARUS

12

Berlin ■

Warsaw ■

GERMANY

POLAND

Kiev ■

Brussels ■

BELGIUM

8

4

UKRAINE

5

Paris ■

SLOVAKIA

1

Vienna ■ ■ Bratislava

MOLDOVA

FRANCE

15

AUSTRIA

■ Budapest

■ Chisinau

7

HUNGARY

ITALY

14

3

ROMANIA

2

11

13

2

Belgrade ■

■ Bucharest

YUGOSLAVIA

BULGARIA

Rome ■

16

■ Sofia

Tirana ■

9

ALBANIA

4

GREECE

■ Athens

10

CYPRUS   ■ Nicosia

1. **ANDORRA**
   Andorra le Vella
2. **BOSNIA-HERZEGOVINA**
   Sarajevo
3. **CROATIA**
   Zagreb
4. **CZECH REPUBLIC**
   Prague
5. **ICELAND**
   Reykjavik
6. **Kaliningrad**
   (belongs to Russia)
7. **LIECHTENSTEIN**
   Vaduz
8. **LUXEMBOURG**
   Luxembourg
9. **MACEDONIA**
   Skopje
10. **MALTA**
    Valletta
11. **MONACO**
    Monaco
12. **NETHERLANDS**
    Amsterdam,
    The Hague
13. **SAN MARINO**
    San Marino
14. **SLOVENIA**
    Ljubljana
15. **SWITZERLAND**
    Bern
16. **VATICAN CITY**
    Vatican City

Asia

Asia is big in many ways. It is the biggest continent, covering a third of the world's land area. It also has the biggest population by far – nearly two-thirds of all the people in the world live in Asia.

Asia also has the biggest range of scenery. It contains the highest place on Earth (Mount Everest) and the lowest (the Dead Sea), as well as deserts, jungles and frozen plains. There are vast stretches of empty land which is no good for farming, but there are also river valleys which have some of the best farmland anywhere in the world.

◀ The black woodpecker has the loudest tap in the world! It can be heard up to 1.8 kilometres away!

Caspian Sea

Mediterranean Sea

Tig

Euphrates Riv

Red Sea

Arabian Peninsula

▲ The Siberian tiger is the largest big cat in the world. It is also the rarest as there are probably only a few hundred left in the wild.

Best of Asia

FRESHWATER SEALS
The Lake Baikal seals are the world's only freshwater seals.

HIGHEST MOUNTAIN
Mount Everest, on China and Nepal's borders, is 8,863 metres high.

LOWEST PLACE
The Dead Sea is situated 400 metres below sea level.

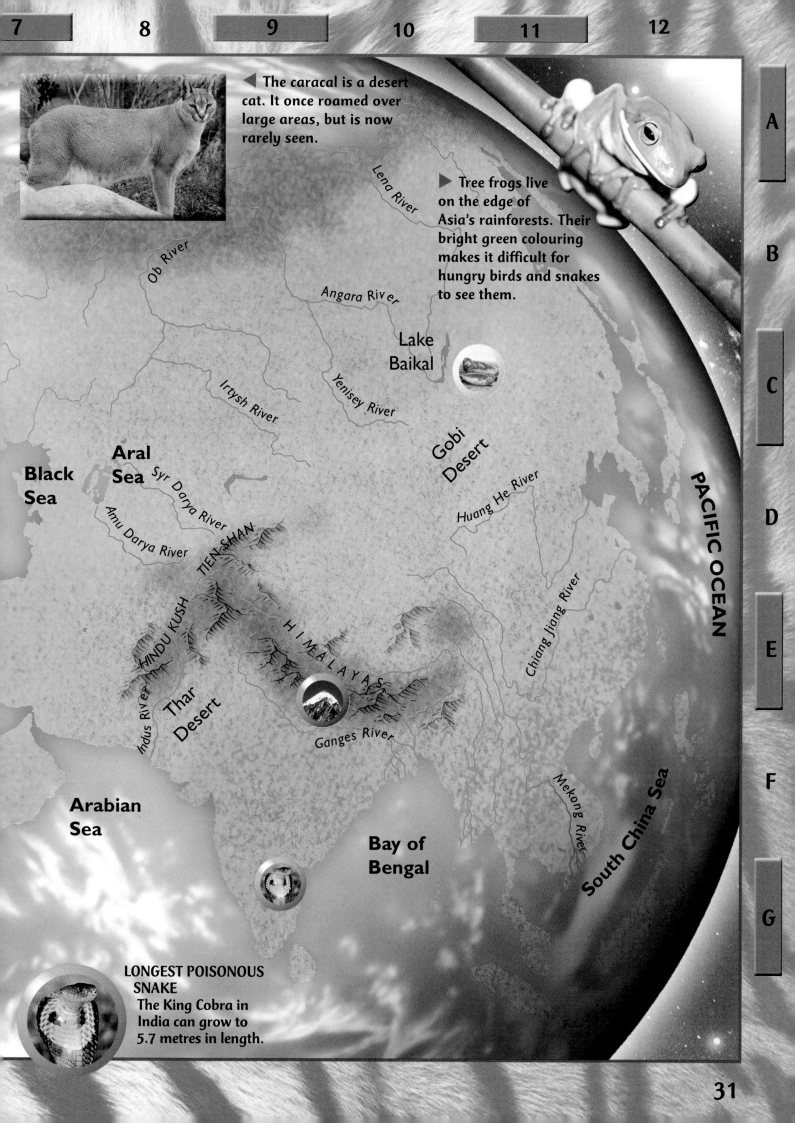

A

B

C

D

E

F

G

◀ The caracal is a desert cat. It once roamed over large areas, but is now rarely seen.

▶ Tree frogs live on the edge of Asia's rainforests. Their bright green colouring makes it difficult for hungry birds and snakes to see them.

Lena River

Ob River

Angara River

Lake Baikal

Irtysh River

Yenisey River

Gobi Desert

PACIFIC OCEAN

Black Sea

Aral Sea

Syr Darya River

Amu Darya River

HINDU KUSH

TIEN SHAN

HIMALAYAS

Huang He River

Chiang Jiang River

Indus River

Thar Desert

Ganges River

Arabian Sea

Mekong River

South China Sea

Bay of Bengal

LONGEST POISONOUS SNAKE
The King Cobra in India can grow to 5.7 metres in length.

Asia
People and places

Asia contains a huge number of different races.

Each speaks a different language and follows a different way of life. There are Mongolian herdsmen living on the vast grasslands, and city-dwellers living in modern Japan. Oil brings wealth to many Arab people, while most people in India work on small farms. Big cities such as Tokyo are among the most crowded in the world. The world's major religions – Christianity, Islam and Hinduism – all began in Asia.

▲ Mongolian people live on the grassland steppes of central Asia, where they raise herds of goats, cattle and yaks. They live in felt-covered tents called yurts.

Asia Facts

Biggest country Russia – 13,400,000 square kilometres (in Asia, the rest of Russia is in Europe)

Biggest country population
China – 1,283,570,000 people

Biggest city population
Tokyo, Japan – 27,242,000 people

Most children in a family
Yemen – an average of 8

Longest railway line Trans-Siberia line – 9,297 kilometres (part of which is in Europe)

TURKEY

Ankara ■

①   13
    19
9 10

8

11
4
16
Riyadh ■
SAUDI ARABIA

Sana ■
YEMEN

▲ In India and other Asian countries, bicycles are used as taxis. These taxis are called rickshaws – they are also used for moving heavy goods about.

◀ Muslims believe that the Dome of the Rock in Jerusalem is the holiest place on Earth. It was built over the rock from which, according to Muslim belief, Muhammad rose to heaven.

▶ China holds a New Year's Day parade. A group of people dress up in a large dragon costume. They believe that the dragon helps prevent evil spirits from spoiling the New Year.

④

QUIZ
1. Which one country would you have to travel through to get from Iran to India?
2. Mongolia shares a border with two other countries, what are they?
Answers on page 48.

A
B
C
D
E
F
G

1. **AFGHANISTAN** Kabul
2. **ARMENIA** Yerevan
3. **AZERBAIJAN** Baku
4. **BAHRAIN** Manama
5. **BANGLADESH** Dhaka
6. **BHUTAN** Thimphu
7. **GEORGIA** Tbilisi
8. **IRAQ** Baghdad
9. **ISRAEL** Jerusalem
10. **JORDAN** Amman
11. **KUWAIT** Kuwait
12. **KYRGYZSTAN** Bishkek
13. **LEBANON** Beirut
14. **MALDIVES** Male
15. **NORTH KOREA** P'yŏngyang
16. **QATAR** Doha
17. **SINGAPORE** Singapore
18. **SOUTH KOREA** Seoul
19. **SYRIA** Damascus
20. **TAJIKISTAN** Dushanbe
21. **TURKMENISTAN** Ashkhabad
22. **UNITED ARAB EMIRATES** Abu Dhabi
23. **UZBEKISTAN** Tashkent

■ Moscow

RUSSIA

■ Astana
KAZAKHSTAN

Ulan Bator ■ ③
MONGOLIA

JAPAN
Tokyo ■

15

18

Beijing ■

7
2
3

21   23

Tehran   12

20

IRAN

1

CHINA

⑤

④

■ Islamabad

PAKISTAN

NEPAL
Kathmandu ■
6

T'aipei ■
TAIWAN

■ Muscat
OMAN

Delhi ■

5

② **INDIA**

MYANMAR (BURMA)
Rangoon (Yangon) ■

LAOS
■ Hanoi
■ Vientiane

Manila ■
PHILIPPINES

Bangkok ■
THAILAND

VIETNAM
■ Phnom Penh
CAMBODIA

Bandar Seri Begawan ■
BRUNEI

14 ■ Colombo
SRI LANKA

⑤

MALAYSIA
■ Kuala Lumpur
17

◀ This army of terracotta warriors is in the world's largest tomb in China. Qin Shihuangdi's, Emperor of China, was buried here 2,210 years ago.

INDONESIA
■ Jakarta

■ Dili
EAST TIMOR

Africa

Africa is the second biggest continent in the world. You could fit Europe into it nearly three times over! But fewer people live in the whole of Africa than in Europe.

There are many wonderful natural sights in Africa, such as Mount Kilimanjaro and the wildlife of the jungles and grasslands.

The longest river, the Nile, flows through the northeast of the continent. It provides water for the farmland along its banks. But much of Africa is an extremely hot and dry place to live because it lies across the Equator. The largest desert in the world, the Sahara Desert, takes up most of the north of the continent, but there are tropical rainforests further south.

Even though there are plenty of minerals, such as gold, diamonds, and even oil, two-thirds of the world's poorest countries are on the African continent.

The lion is the largest big cat in Africa. It can grow to 3 metres in length.

ATLANTIC OCEAN

▶ The African elephant is the largest land animal in the world. It can grow up to 7.5 metres tall and can weigh as much as 90 adult humans!

Best of Africa

TALLEST MAMMAL The giraffe can grow to a height of 6 metres. Its legs are 1.8 metres long.

HIGHEST MOUNTAIN Kilimanjaro soars to 5,894 metres.

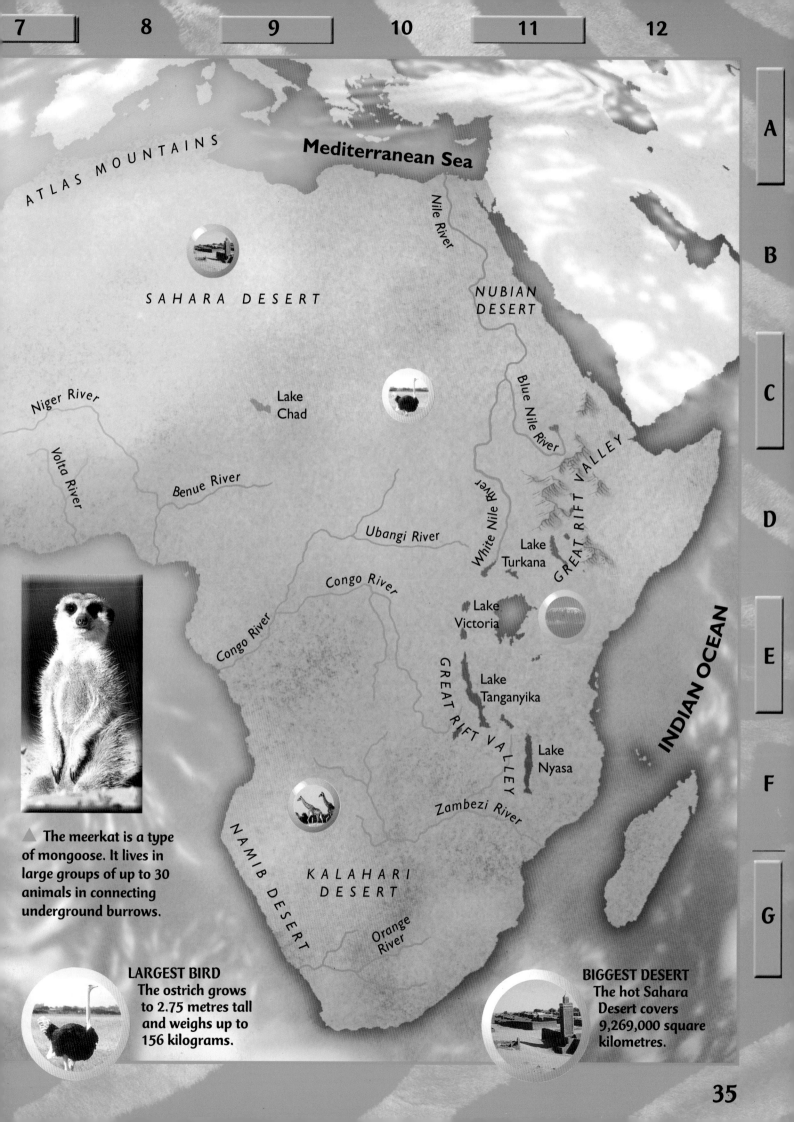

ATLAS MOUNTAINS

Mediterranean Sea

SAHARA DESERT

Nile River

NUBIAN DESERT

Niger River

Lake Chad

Blue Nile River

Volta River

Benue River

White Nile River

GREAT RIFT VALLEY

Ubangi River

Lake Turkana

Congo River

Congo River

Lake Victoria

Lake Tanganyika

GREAT RIFT VALLEY

Lake Nyasa

INDIAN OCEAN

Zambezi River

NAMIB DESERT

KALAHARI DESERT

Orange River

▲ The meerkat is a type of mongoose. It lives in large groups of up to 30 animals in connecting underground burrows.

LARGEST BIRD
The ostrich grows to 2.75 metres tall and weighs up to 156 kilograms.

BIGGEST DESERT
The hot Sahara Desert covers 9,269,000 square kilometres.

Africa People and places

Africa is a very large continent, but it has few people living there.

Nigeria has the biggest population with 108 million people, but a lot of other countries have much smaller populations – less than five million.

African people come from many racial groups. In the north, most are Arabs. South of the Sahara Desert, most people are black. They are divided up into over 800 different groups, each with its own language, religion and way of life.

Very few people live in the deserts or the dry grasslands. The most crowded areas are the Nile Valley, the Algerian coast and the South African coast.

Over 60 percent of Africans live in villages. They grow crops and raise cattle and other animals to feed themselves. This is a hard way of life, because the soil is poor and the climate is harsh.

▲ These children from the Masai tribe live in Kenya. The traditional clothing of the Masai people is a single piece of cloth wrapped around them. These children are wearing traditional decorative beads.

▲ The Bolga people of Ghana paint their houses in bright colours. Most are farmers whose main crop is cacao beans. They sell these beans to other countries who use them to make chocolate!

▼ Camels are still a very important method of transport in Egypt. They are known as 'ships of the desert', and can travel for days without drinking or eating.

Africa Facts

Biggest country Sudan – 2,503,890 square kilometres

Smallest country Seychelles – 455 square kilometres

Biggest city population Cairo, Egypt – 11,600,000 people

Shortest people Pygmies – about 140 centimetres

Largest producer of gold
South Africa – 33 percent of world total

Most children in a family
Niger – an average of 7

Shortest average length of life
Zimbabwe – 39 years

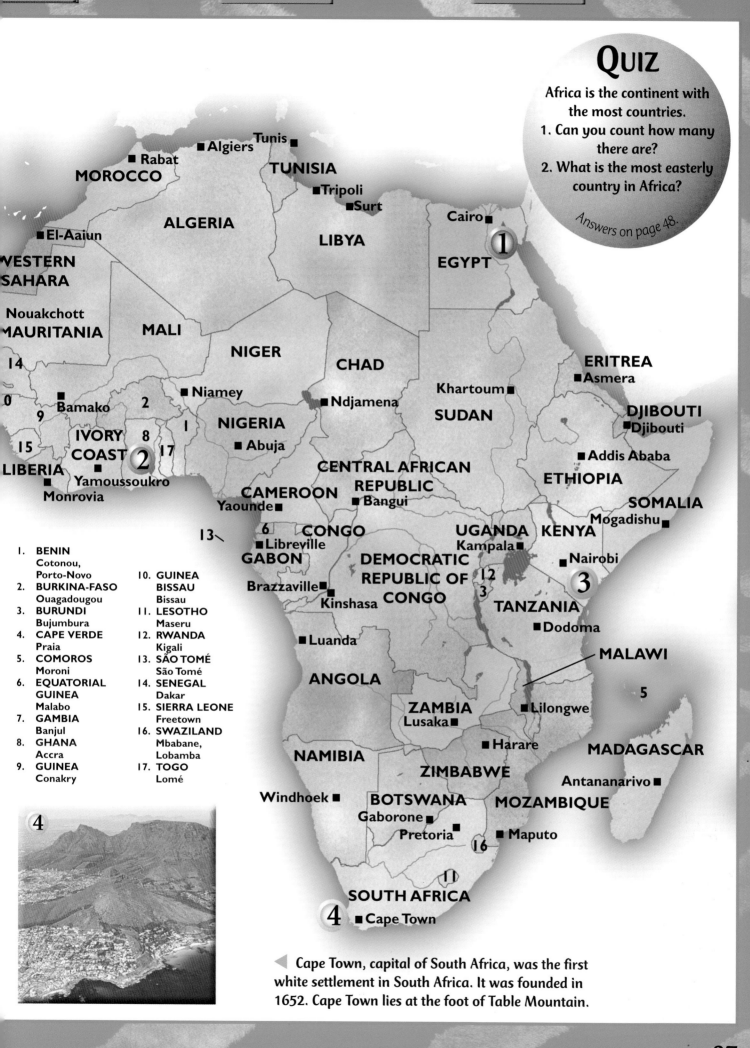

QUIZ

Africa is the continent with the most countries.

1. Can you count how many there are?
2. What is the most easterly country in Africa?

Answers on page 48.

MOROCCO
- Rabat
- Algiers
- Tunis
- El-Aaiun

WESTERN SAHARA

TUNISIA
- Tripoli
- Surt

ALGERIA

LIBYA

- Cairo
EGYPT ①

MAURITANIA
- Nouakchott

MALI
- Bamako

NIGER
- Niamey

CHAD
- Ndjamena

SUDAN
- Khartoum

ERITREA
- Asmera

DJIBOUTI
- Djibouti

14
0
9

2
1

8
17

NIGERIA
- Abuja

IVORY COAST
- Yamoussoukro

15

LIBERIA
- Monrovia

CENTRAL AFRICAN REPUBLIC
- Bangui

ETHIOPIA
- Addis Ababa

CAMEROON
- Yaounde

SOMALIA
- Mogadishu

13

6
- Libreville

CONGO

GABON

UGANDA
- Kampala

KENYA
- Nairobi

DEMOCRATIC REPUBLIC OF CONGO
- Brazzaville
- Kinshasa

12
3

TANZANIA
- Dodoma

MALAWI
- Lilongwe

- Luanda

5

ANGOLA

MADAGASCAR
- Antananarivo

ZAMBIA
- Lusaka

- Harare

NAMIBIA
- Windhoek

ZIMBABWE

MOZAMBIQUE

BOTSWANA
- Gaborone
- Pretoria
- Maputo

16

11

SOUTH AFRICA
④ - Cape Town

Key

1. **BENIN** Cotonou, Porto-Novo
2. **BURKINA-FASO** Ouagadougou
3. **BURUNDI** Bujumbura
4. **CAPE VERDE** Praia
5. **COMOROS** Moroni
6. **EQUATORIAL GUINEA** Malabo
7. **GAMBIA** Banjul
8. **GHANA** Accra
9. **GUINEA** Conakry
10. **GUINEA BISSAU** Bissau
11. **LESOTHO** Maseru
12. **RWANDA** Kigali
13. **SÃO TOMÉ** São Tomé
14. **SENEGAL** Dakar
15. **SIERRA LEONE** Freetown
16. **SWAZILAND** Mbabane, Lobamba
17. **TOGO** Lomé

④

◀ Cape Town, capital of South Africa, was the first white settlement in South Africa. It was founded in 1652. Cape Town lies at the foot of Table Mountain.

Oceania

Oceania is really more than one continent. It is the name we give to a group of islands covering an enormous area in the Pacific Ocean. The biggest of these islands is Australia, and there are 14 other countries. Oceania is the smallest of the continents.

The next biggest parts of Oceania are New Zealand (which is made up of two islands) and Papua New Guinea. The rest of this strange continent is made up of at least 30,000 small islands.

Much of this area has been isolated from the rest of the world for millions of years, so many unique animals are found here. Animals like the duck-billed platypus, the kangaroo and the koala are found nowhere else in the world.

▲ Koalas are only found in Australia. They are covered with soft, thick brown and grey fur. They eat the leaves and young shoots of eucalyptus trees.

INDIAN OCEAN

▲ The duck-billed platypus is one of the strangest mammals in the world. It has fur like a mammal, but it has webbed feet like a duck. It also has a bill like a bird, and it lays eggs!

▼ Ayers Rock, now called Uluru, in Australia is the largest free-standing rock in the world. It is 300 metres high and over 600 million years old.

Best of Oceania

LARGEST BUTTERFLY
Queen Alexandra's birdwing has a wingspan of 280 millimetres.

LONGEST CORAL REEF
The Great Barrier Reef in Australia is 2,025 kilometres long.

OLDEST ROCKS
Zircon crystals from Australia are 4,276 billion years old.

A

B

C

D

E

F

G

▶ The beautiful mountainous island of Moorea lies in the South Pacific. The warm temperatures rarely fall below 21 degrees Celsius.

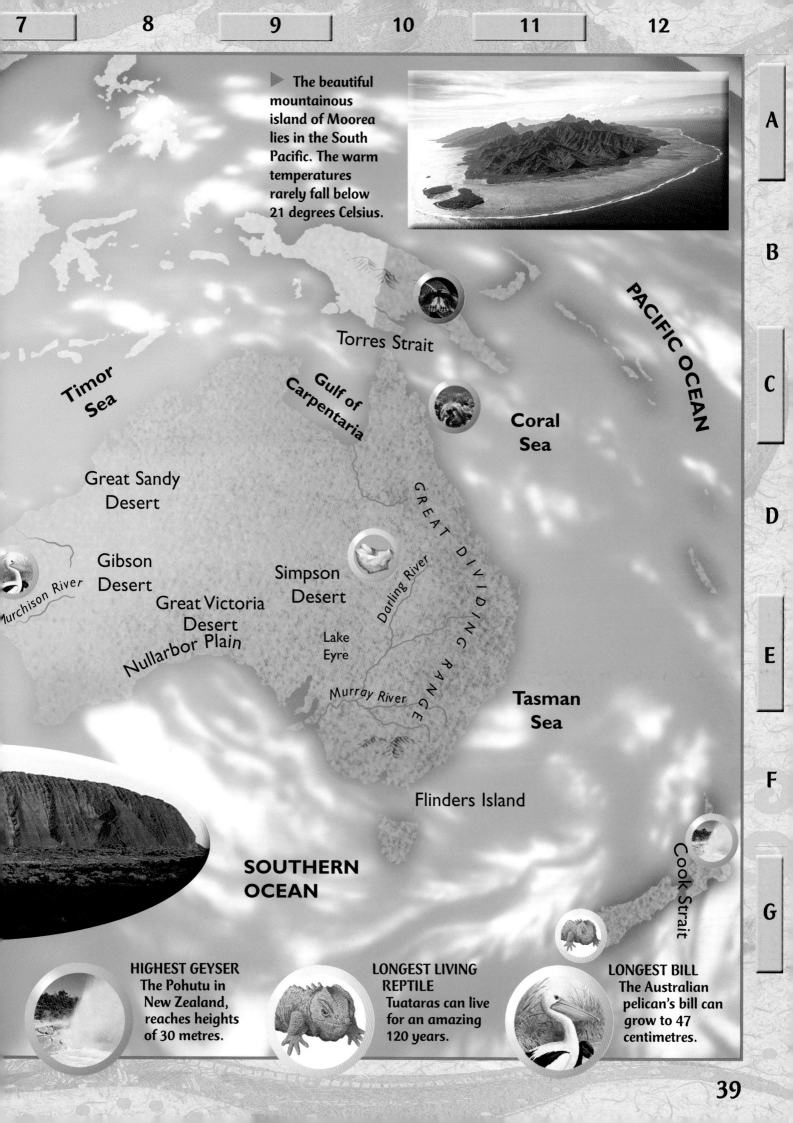

PACIFIC OCEAN

Torres Strait

Timor Sea

Gulf of Carpentaria

Coral Sea

Great Sandy Desert

Gibson Desert

Murchison River

Great Victoria Desert

Nullarbor Plain

Simpson Desert

Lake Eyre

Darling River

GREAT DIVIDING RANGE

Murray River

Tasman Sea

Flinders Island

Cook Strait

SOUTHERN OCEAN

HIGHEST GEYSER
The Pohutu in New Zealand, reaches heights of 30 metres.

LONGEST LIVING REPTILE
Tuataras can live for an amazing 120 years.

LONGEST BILL
The Australian pelican's bill can grow to 47 centimetres.

Oceania People and places

About 80 percent of Australians live in the south-east corner. Nearly all the major cities are here, including the capital, Canberra. The land is good for farming and the climate is mild and wet. Almost nobody lives in the centre of the country, known as the outback. It consists of vast deserts and grasslands.

Most Australians come from families that moved here from Europe during the 20th century. Aboriginals, the first people to live in Australia, now make up less than one percent of the total. However, it was not always like this. Aboriginals, like the other first people of Oceania, travelled from Southeast Asia 40,000 to 70,000 years ago. They sailed from island to island for thousands of years, setting up homes in many places. When the British came to Australia 200 years ago they destroyed the Aboriginals' way of life.

Farming and mining make Australia and New Zealand wealthy countries, and Papua New Guinea produces timber and copper. The smaller countries have little to sell and are much poorer. However, the tourist industry is growing fast in the Pacific and this is helping to create jobs and bring money to the islands.

QUIZ

Many places in Oceania take their name from early explorers who came from Europe. Can you find on the map on page 39 places named after: James Cook, Abel Tasman Matthew Flinders, Luis de Torres Edward Eyre?

Answers on page 48.

Oceania Facts

Biggest country Australia – 7,700,000 square kilometres

Smallest country Nauru – 21 square kilometres

Biggest city population Sydney, Australia – 3,900,000 people

Longest average length of life Australia – 78 years

Country that produces most diamonds Australia – 34 percent of the world total

▶ **The Sydney Opera House** looks over the harbour in Australia. The building was finished in 1973.

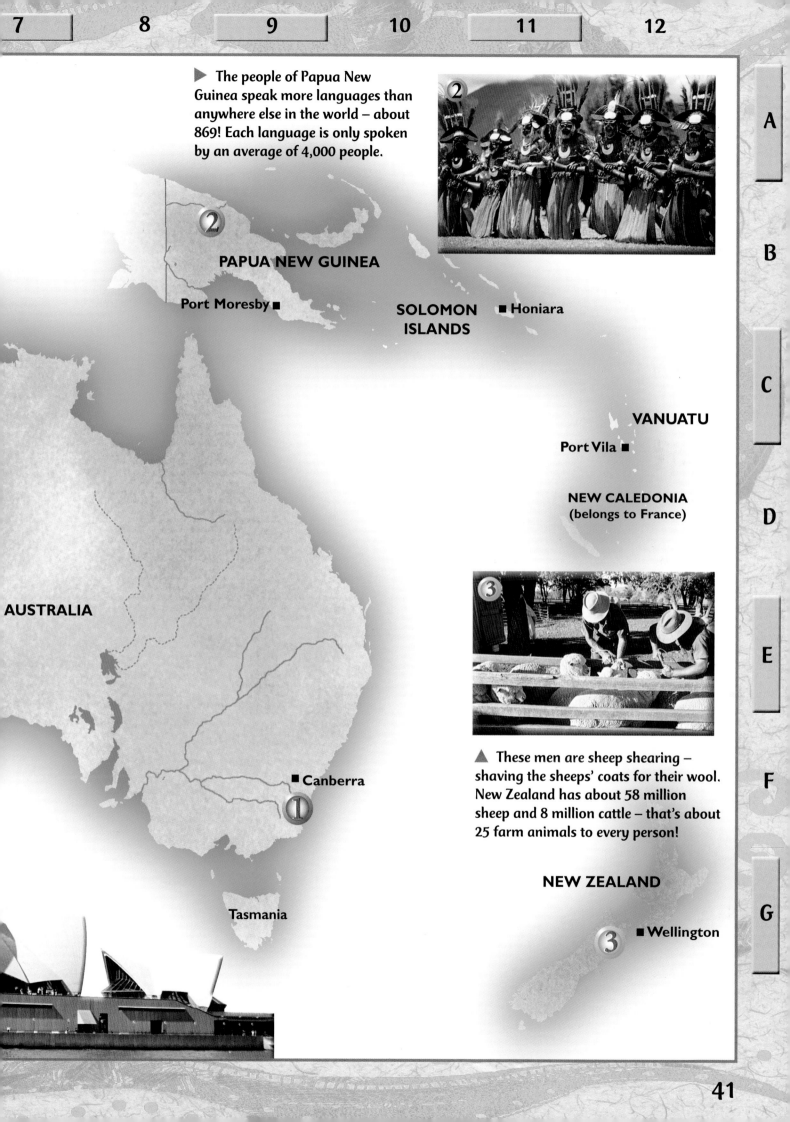

▶ The people of Papua New Guinea speak more languages than anywhere else in the world – about 869! Each language is only spoken by an average of 4,000 people.

② PAPUA NEW GUINEA

Port Moresby ■

SOLOMON ISLANDS　■ Honiara

VANUATU

Port Vila ■

NEW CALEDONIA
(belongs to France)

AUSTRALIA

■ Canberra

①

Tasmania

③ These men are sheep shearing – shaving the sheeps' coats for their wool. New Zealand has about 58 million sheep and 8 million cattle – that's about 25 farm animals to every person!

NEW ZEALAND

③ ■ Wellington

41

Antarctica

Antarctica is the most difficult place to live in the world. It is the coldest continent, and 98 percent of the land area is covered with ice and snow. Some of the ice is nearly five kilometres deep – more than ten times the height of the world's tallest building! The ice reaches out into the sea forming huge ice shelves that occasionally break off to form vast floating icebergs.

Almost nothing grows here, so it is not surprising that Antarctica has the smallest population in the world – exactly 0! However, a few explorers and tourists visit, and there are several camps where scientists work studying animals and the ice.

Even animals find it difficult to live here. The few that do, live mainly in the air or in the sea. Penguins, seals and whales survive because of their thick layer of blubber, or fat, which keeps them warm. They feed off fish and tiny animals called krill that live in the sea.

▲ The first person to reach the South Pole was Norwegian Roald Amundsen in 1911. This museum is dedicated to him and the British explorer, Captain Scott, the man he beat to the pole.

▲ The albatross has the largest wingspan of any living bird. Its wings measure 3.6 metres across!

Best of Antarctica

COLDEST PLACE
Vostok Station, on July 21, 1983, recorded −89.2 degrees Celsius.

DEEPEST ICE
Ice has been found to a depth of 4,776 metres.

◄ The Weddell seal from Antarctica is one of the largest seals in the world, growing up to 2.9 metres long. It makes deeper and longer dives than any other seal. It has been recorded underwater for 73 minutes diving to a depth of 600 metres.

QUIZ

Which of these animals live in the Antarctic?
Polar bear
Emperor penguin
Arctic tern
weddell seal
Albatross
Answers on page 48.

SOUTH PACIFIC OCEAN

SOUTH ATLANTIC OCEAN

Weddell Sea

Ronne Ice Shelf

■ Halley Station (UK)

Ross Ice Shelf

o South Pole

■ McMurdo Air Station (USA)

Molodezhnaya ■ Station (Russia)

West Antarctica

Dumont D'Urville Station (France) ■

Vostok Station (Russia)

■ Casey Base (Australia)

INDIAN OCEAN

► The emperor penguin is the largest of all penguins, reaching a height of 1.2 metres. It raises its young on the Antarctic ice, enduring severe cold and winds.

| A | B | C | D | E | F | G |

43

CAPITAL CITIES OF THE WORLD

These are all the countries of the world and their capital cities. You will see that some countries have two capital cities.

North America

Antigua and Barbuda	St John's
Bahamas	Nassau
Barbados	Bridgetown
Belize	Belmopan
Canada	Ottawa
Costa Rica	San Jose
Cuba	Havana
Dominica	Roseau
Dominican Republic	Santo Domingo
El Salvador	San Salvador
Grenada	St George's
Guatemala	Guatemala
Haiti	Port-au-Prince
Honduras	Tegucigalpa
Jamaica	Kingston
Mexico	Mexico City
Nicaragua	Managua
Panama	Panama
St Kitts-Nevis	Basseterre
St Lucia	Castries
St Pierre and Miquelon	St Pierre
St Vincent and the Grenadines	Kingstown
Trinidad and Tobago	Port-of-Spain
United States of America	Washington D.C.

South America

Argentina	Buenos Aires
Bolivia	La Paz
Brazil	Brasília
Chile	Santiago
Colombia	Bogota
Ecuador	Quito
Guyana	Georgetown
Paraguay	Asunción
Peru	Lima
Suriname	Paramaribo
Uruguay	Montevideo
Venezuela	Caracas

Europe

Albania	Tirané
Andorra	Andorra le Vella
Austria	Vienna
Belarus	Minsk
Belgium	Brussels
Bosnia-Herzegovina	Sarajevo
Bulgaria	Sofia
Croatia	Zagreb
Cyprus	Nicosia
Czech Republic	Prague
Denmark	Copenhagen
England	London
Estonia	Tallinn
Finland	Helsinki
France	Paris
Germany	Berlin
Greece	Athens
Hungary	Budapest
Iceland	Reykjavik
Ireland	Dublin
Italy	Rome
Latvia	Riga
Liechtenstein	Vaduz
Lithuania	Vilnius
Luxembourg	Luxembourg
Macedonia	Skopje
Malta	Valletta
Moldova	Chisinau
Monaco	Monaco
Netherlands	Amsterdam, The Hague
Norway	Oslo
Poland	Warsaw
Portugal	Lisbon
Romania	Bucharest
Russia	Moscow
San Marino	San Marino
Scotland	Edinburgh
Slovakia	Bratislava
Slovenia	Ljubljana
Spain	Madrid
Sweden	Stockholm
Switzerland	Bern
Ukraine	Kiev
Vatican City	Vatican City
Wales	Cardiff
Yugoslavia	Belgrade

Asia

Afghanistan	Kabul
Armenia	Yerevan
Azerbaijan	Baku
Bahrain	Manama
Bangladesh	Dhaka
Bhutan	Thimphu
Brunei	Bandar Seri Begawan
Cambodia	Phnom Penh
China	Beijing (Peking)
East Timor	Dili
Georgia	Tbilisi
India	Delhi
Indonesia	Jakarta
Iran	Tehran
Iraq	Baghdad

Israel	Jerusalem	Burkina-Faso	Ouagadougou	Sierra Leone	Freetown
Japan	Tokyo	Burundi	Bujumbura	Somalia	Mogadishu
Jordan	Amman	Cameroon	Yaoundé	South Africa	Cape Town,
Kazakhstan	Astana	Cape Verde	Praia		Pretoria
Kuwait	Kuwait	Central African		Sudan	Khartoum
Kyrgyzstan	Bishkek	Republic	Bangui	Swaziland	Lobamba,
Laos	Vientiane	Chad	N'Djamena		Mbabane
Lebanon	Beirut	Comoros	Moroni	Tanzania	Dodoma
Malaysia	Kuala Lumpur	Congo	Brazzaville	Togo	Lomé
Maldives	Male	Côte D'Ivoire	Yamoussoukro	Tunisia	Tunis
Mongolia	Ulaanbaatar	Democratic Republic		Uganda	Kampala
Myanmar (Burma)	Yangon	of Congo	Kinshasa	Western Sahara	El-Aaiun
	(Rangoon)	Djibouti	Djibouti	Zambia	Lusaka
Nepal	Kathmandu	Egypt	Cairo	Zimbabwe	Harare
North Korea	P'yŏngyang	Equatorial Guinea	Malabo		
Oman	Muscat	Eritrea	Asmera		

Oceania

Pakistan	Islamabad	Ethiopia	Addis Ababa	Australia	Canberra
Philippines	Manila	Gabon	Libreville	Federated States	
Qatar	Doha	Gambia	Banjul	of Micronesia	Palikir
Saudi Arabia	Riyadh	Ghana	Accra	Fiji	Suva
Singapore	Singapore	Guinea	Conakry	Kiribati	Bairiki
South Korea	Seoul	Guinea-Bissau	Bissau	Marshall Islands	Dalap-Uliga-
Sri Lanka	Colombo, Kotte	Kenya	Nairobi		Darrit
Syria	Damascus	Lesotho	Maseru	Nauru	Yangor
Taiwan	T'aipei	Liberia	Monrovia	New Zealand	Wellington
Tajikistan	Dushanbe	Libya	Tripoli, Surt	Palau	Koror
Thailand	Bangkok	Madagascar	Antananarivo	Papua New Guinea	Port Moresby
Turkey	Ankara	Malawi	Lilongwe	Soloman Islands	Honiara
Turkmenistan	Ashkhabad	Mali	Bamako	Tonga	Nuku'alofa
United Arab Emirates	Abu Dhabi	Mauritania	Nouakchott	Tuvalu	Fongafale
Uzbekistan	Tashkent	Mauritius	Port Louis	Vanuatu	Port Vila
Vietnam	Hanoi	Morocco	Rabat	Western Samoa	Apia
Yemen	Sanaa	Mozambique	Maputo		
		Namibia	Windhoek		

Africa

Algeria	Algiers	Niger	Niamey	
Angola	Luanda	Nigeria	Abuja	
Benin	Cotonou,	Rwanda	Kigali	
	Porto-Novo	São Tomé	São Tomé	
Botswana	Gaborone	Senegal	Dakar	
		Seychelles	Victoria	

INDEX

46

QUIZ ANSWERS

Page 13

1. Asia
2. Oceania
3. Asia
4. Antarctica
5. Africa

Page 20

D10 Ottawa
G9 Mexico City
E11 Washington D.C.
F11 Nassau

Page 24

1. 12
2. Brasilia (capital of Brazil)

Page 29

Scotland (OLD SCANT)
Denmark (MARK END)
Russia (SIR USA)
Germany (ANGRY ME)
Britain (RAIN BIT)
France (CAR FEN)

Page 33

1. Pakistan
2. Russia and China

Page 37

1. 53
2. Somalia

Page 40

Cook Straight G12
Tasman Sea E11
Flinders Island F10
Torres Strait C10
Lake Eyre E9

Page 43

Emperor penguin
Weddell seal
Albatross